Ramana.
Essence of.
(Upadesa _ain):

The Pine Forest Revisited

translated from Sanskrit,
with commentary
by
Miles Wright

translation of the six verses of Introduction
from Tamil
by Sri Suri Suryanarayan

ed. by Gabriele Ebert

FSC
www.fsc.org

MIX

Papier aus ver-
antwortungsvollen
Quellen
Paper from
responsible sources

FSC® C105338

Ramana Maharshi:
The Essence of Instruction (Upadesa Saram):
The Pine Forest Revisited
2. ed. 2014

Herstellung und Verlag:
BoD – Books on Demand, Norderstedt
ISBN 978-3-7386-0091-9

Umschlaggestaltung: BoD
Foto: Sri Ramanasramam
Printed in Germany

Table of Contents

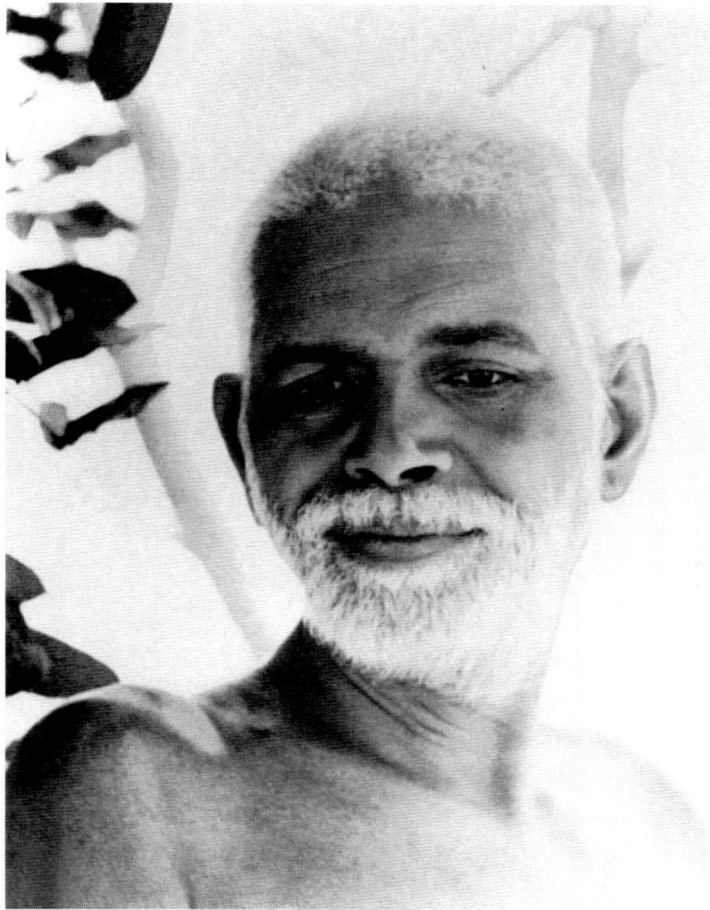

Preface

There is an old legend about the Rishis (wise men) who lived in a pine forest together with their wives. They practiced the ritual rites of the Karma Kanda, a book of the Vedas. As a result of their practices, they attained supernatural powers and, in this way, they expected to gain liberation. But, in truth, their practices bolstered the arrogance of their egos. At this point, Siva appeared on the scene and taught them a painful lesson which showed the absurdity of their puffed up attitudes. Having been humbled the Rishis became open for instruction. Siva taught them, in his mercy, the correct way to attain the natural state of the Self.

The Tamil-poet Muruganar, a well respected devotee of Ramana Maharshi, wanted to write a hundred verses about this legend. But when he completed 70 verses he could not proceed and requested that Bhagavan Sri Ramana Maharshi take over that part of the story which dealt with Siva's teaching to the Rishis. Sri Ramana wrote the missing 30 verses in Tamil as Upadesa Undiyar, which he later translated into Sanskrit as Upadesa Saram ("nectar or essence of instruction").

These 30 verses are the quintessence of Sri Ramana's teaching. In their significance they are comparable to the old Upanishads. During the lifetime of Ramana, they were recited daily in the hall in his presence. This habit continues down to today at Ramanashram.

Miles Wright has translated these 30 verses from Sanskrit into English with apposite comments.

Introduction to Upadesa Saram

1. The Rishis who were doing tapas in dAruvanam went astray because of their pUrva karmA.

2. Steeped in ignorance with deceitful pride, they believed that there is no God other than karmA.

In the Heart-lotus of each and every one, Bhagavan dances the eternal dance of the Self. This, in essence, is the rhythm of existence; felt as the *sphurana* 'I-I', or ... Being. At times one might lose sight of this simple fact. And, when this happens, the illusion of free-will will appear to take hold. Even the great *Rishis* of Darukavanam (The Pine Forest) were not exempt from the illusion of independence. Although they were extremely adept at the Karma Kanda or ritualistic section of the Veda, which deals with Yajnas (sacrificial rites) etc., and despite the intensity of their Vedic ritual and ceremonial, indeed, because of the performance of their Yajnas, their egos had become puffed up to a very great extent. The rituals had, in fact, become counter-productive because they merely provided fuel for the great fire of pride that the *Rishis* had in their own egocentric abilities. They had become hooked on action and every attainment threw up the desire for a further bigger, better attainment. Things have not changed much since then ... have they? The human condition continues to be enthralled with the shadows all the while oblivious to the all important source of the light.

3. They realized the fruits of abusing God, the kartA, who ordains the fruits of karma. Their pride (arrogance) left them.

Having observed the misunderstandings of the *Rishis*, and in order to show them that *karma* was definitely not the means to an end, Lord Siva appeared in the forest hermitage in the guise of a religious mendicant, along with Lord Vishnu, who had taken, at the request of Lord Siva, the guise of a beautiful girl, named Mohini.

The disguised pair, mendicant monk and beautiful girl, wandered towards the centre of the busy hermitage. The *Rishis* were householders and lived with their wives. When the wives of the *Rishis* saw the Mendicant Siva, they at once fell in love with Him. The wives' hearts were captivated, their husbands were forgotten. At the same time, as soon as the *Rishis* laid eyes on Mohini, they became completely infatuated with Her. Everywhere She went they followed unable to control their senses. Despite their intense forest *tapas*, passion took hold of the *Rishis'* minds and this was soon joined by a fierce anger, when they observed the state of their wives. An anger which they vowed to unleash on the Mendicant (Lord Siva) using all the powers at their disposal. They began an enormous sacrificial fire, in a very deep pit, and performed all the appropriate *mantras*. In their pride they thought that they would easily defeat the impertinent Mendicant. They conjured up a fierce man-eating tiger which they sent after the Mendicant. He simply grabbed it and wrapped it around His waist. They conjured up a rogue elephant which immediately charged at the Mendicant. He took it in one hand and slung it over His shoulder as a cloak. Then they created poisonous snakes which the Mendicant took as belt, necklaces and amulets. Even a charmed trident went straight into the hand of the Mendicant. Weapon after weapon became an ornament of the Mendicant Siva and the *Rishis* of the Pine Forest fell down on their knees, then onto their fronts, exhausted physically and mentally, all passion, anger, greed, attachment and pride had finally subsided, and they beseeched the Mendicant to reveal His true Form that they might be instructed by such a great Sage. Their egoism no longer in the way they were at last open to instruction. Lord Siva revealed Himself.

4. When they prayed to Him to save them (in humility) Siva
blessed them with karuNa filled eyes.
This is Siva's upadESa.

It was at this point in the story that the great Tamil poet Muruganar approached Bhagavan Sri Ramana Maharshi and requested elucidation on the Instruction which had been given by Lord Siva to the *Rishis*. Bhagavan agreed and wrote the Instruction in 30 verses. Later the verses were translated into Telugu, Malayalam and, at the request of the great Sanskritist, Kavyakantha Ganapati

Muni, they were also translated into Sanskrit. This current work is a translation from the Sanskrit verses.

> *5. If one lives by this sAram of Siva's upadESa, all sorrows will disapear and joy will fill the heart.*

This *upadesa* is indeed Siva's *Upadesa*, repeated once again by Him, at the request of His devotee, while living on the holy Mount Arunachala.

> *6. Hence, may the sAram of this upadESa fill our heart. May bliss swell; May sorrows be exhausted.*

It has been said by some commentators on Upadesa Saram that the verses of Bhagavan Sri Ramana Maharshi are terse and difficult to understand because of 'cryptic style'. This is undoubtedly not the case. All comments made herein by the writer are but apposite notes and observations which have come out of conversations and close reading and which may aid in the Quest.

Thank you to the devotion of Sri Muruganar for giving impetus to these Upadesa Saram verses which reveal the essence of Vedanta as revealed through the direct, ever-radiant, Self-experience of the Sage of Arunachala.

> *jyotishAmapi tajjyotistamasah paramucyate /*
> *jnAnam jneyam jnAnagamyam hrdi sarvasya vishThitam //*

> "Light of lights, beyond the darkness, He is called; true knowledge, that which is to be known, understood through knowledge, abiding in the Heart of all."
> (Bhagavad Gita, 13; 17)

> "That which is the source of all, that in which all live, and that in-to which all finally merge, is the heart referred to [in verse 10 of Upadesa Saram]."
> (Day by Day; 29-4-46)

Upadesa Saram

1.

ॐ

karturAjnayA prApyatephalam /
karmakimparamkarmatajjaDam //

**The fruit (of action) is ordained by the order of the Lord
of Action (Creator). Is action supreme? (No!!) Action is
inert.**

Notes

Action, although a power of the Self, is, by itself, insentient, temporary, and powerless. As such, action is unable to bestow fruits now
or at any time in the future. Action is dependent. It is not supreme.
The *'kartr'* (Lord of Action), referred to in this verse, is the 'one
who acts, spontaneously, of his own accord, without prompting by
the ego' (i.e. the great non-Doer). It is the Lord alone, dwelling as
the inner Self of all, who guides everything yet never acts. If you
believe that you are the person, capable of acting independently,
the chain of cause and effect, having been set in motion, becomes
your reality. As the doer of action you become accountable for action and also the recipient of the fruits of that action. This misunderstanding of the true state of affairs results in the human condition. Ritual action (worship for appeasement) is of this sort.

In Talks, Yogi Ramiah questions Sri Ramana on the nature of action.

> Yogi Ramiah: All actions take place owing to *Sakti*. How far
> does *Sakti* go? Can she effect anything without one's own effort?
> Maharshi: The answer to the question depends on what *Puru-
> sha* is understood to be. Is he ego or the Self?
> D.: *Purusha* is *svarupa*.

11

M.: But he cannot make any *prayatna* (effort).

D.: *Jiva* is the one who makes the effort.

M.: So long as egoity lasts *prayatna* is necessary. When egoity ceases to be, actions become spontaneous. The ego acts in the presence of the Self. He cannot exist without the Self.

The Self makes the universe what it is by His *Sakti*, and yet He does not Himself act. Sri Krishna says in the Bhagavad Gita, 'I am not the doer and yet actions go on.' It is clear from the Mahabharata that very wonderful actions were effected by Him. Yet He says that He is not the doer. It is like the sun and the world actions.

D.: He is without *abhimana* (attachment) whereas the *jiva* is with *abhimana*.

M.: Yes. Being attached, he acts and also reaps the fruits. If the fruits are according to his desire he is happy; otherwise he is miserable. Happiness and misery are due to his attachment. If the actions were to take place without attachment there would be no expectation of fruit.

D.: Can actions take place spontaneously without individual effort? Should we not cook our food in order to eat it later?

M.: *Atman* acts through the ego. All actions are due to efforts only. A sleeping child is fed by its mother. The child eats food without being wide awake and then denies having taken food in sleep. However the mother knows what happened. Similarly the *jnani* acts unawares. Others see him act, but he does not know it himself. Owing to fear of Him wind blows, etc. That is the order of things. He ordains everything and the universe acts accordingly, yet He does not know. Therefore He is called the great Doer. Every embodied being (*ahamkari*) is bound by *niyama*. Even Brahma cannot transgress it. (Talk 467)

phalamata upapatteh
"From Him (the Lord) are the fruits of actions,
for that (alone) is possible."
(Brahma Sutras 3.2.37)

2.

ॐ

krtimahodadhau patanakAraNam /
phalamaSASvatam gatinirodhakam //

**That transient fruit, which obstructs the way, is the cause
of (further) descent into the great ocean of action.**

Notes

That activity which is made in order to satisfy a 'want' is based on
two things, the desire to possess that which is not possessed, and
the fear of non-attainment of that which is desired. Both the attainment of the desire and the non-attainment of the desire are
equally bitter fruits. From this, linear progression is assured.
Whether there is attainment or non-attainment, the descent, into
the great ocean of action, is continued. Desire for pleasure and fear
of pain come hand in hand and always result in bondage. If you
hold on to pleasure, you will always fear pain. True happiness involves neither of these, ... and That (*Ananda* – true happiness) is
your essence, ... simply dropping one of them releases the bonds of
both. This happens as soon as you realise that all this is just
mindstuff. The idea that this action will give that effect is
mindstuff.

These 'things', that you think you do, are not done by you. Things,
apparently, happen, but where are you? What is your role? Your
involvement is mindstuff. Action with desire for result is mindstuff.
In this verse, Sri Ramana says that this is the obstruction.

"One should not be elated on having his desire fulfilled or dis-
appointed on being frustrated. To be elated on the fulfilment of
desire is so deceitful. A gain will certainly be lost ultimately.
Therefore elation must end in pain at a future date. One should
not give place to feelings of pleasure or pain, come what may.
How do the events affect the person? You do not grow by ac-

quiring something nor wither away by losing it. You remain what you always are." (Talk 614)

Remember, ... you are not the mind ... but even so ... this mind appears to have the power to enslave or liberate.

3.

ॐ

ISvaraArptiam necchayAkrtam /
cittaSodhakam muktisAdhakam //

Action without desire, dedicated to the Lord, purifies the mind and brings about Liberation.

Notes

Ahamkara (ego), acting through self- interest, enslaves. This is a poor reflection of genuine Self- interest. Genuine Self- interest leads to Peace absolute. The desire for gain, on the other hand, creates a chain of mental unrest which doesn't stop with the attainment of one object of desire, but is replaced, after fulfilment or otherwise, and subsequent pleasure or pain, by another object, then another and another. If you remain within this chain of events, there is no end to desire. If you continue to look outside of yourself to gain the 'things' which are expected to bring the fruition of happiness then this search will be a never-ending labour.

Instead, Sri Ramana advises the sure course of "action without desire, dedicated to the Lord". This is the way to eliminate mental unrest and purify the mind. Identify with the underlying current. Abandon the false notion that 'I' am acting. Dedicate your life to Arunachala-Ramana. The Self acts through 'I'. Let this action go on. It only happens according to *prarabdha*. There is a store of action which will exhaust itself (even when the electricity is switched off, the fan continues to revolve for a while). Leave it to His devices. The Lord governs all fruits of *karma*. Dedicate all actions to Him, whatever you call Him. Keep Him in the background at all times. Then the sense of 'I am the doer' falls away in favour of 'I am the Instrument of the Lord'.

"Actions form no bondage. Bondage is only the false notion, 'I am the doer'. Leave off such thoughts and let the body and senses play their role, unimpeded by your interference." (Talk 46)

When forgetfulness of the Self brings a feeling of great anguish, then *Atma vicAra* cuts in. When *Atma vicAra* cuts into meandering thoughts at the earliest opportunity then true dedication begins.

With the elimination of desire, identification with the body/mind complex is brought to an end, and the limited individual consciousness naturally returns to the eternal ocean of universal consciousness. The ego might be seen to continue to act, but thought and action no longer pander after the 'wants' of the individual but merely attend to the 'needs'. As the cooling wind blows for the benefit of all in the vicinity so the real man of action adds to the prosperity of the world.

In Bhagavad Gita there is the following description of one who has given up all notion of the false 'I' yet still acts (i.e. the karma yogi).

yadRcchAlAbhasamtushTo dvanvdvAtIto
vimatsarah /
samah siddhAvasiddhau ca krtvApi na
nibadhyate //

"Content with whatever comes, without effort, free from the pairs of opposites, free from envy and even minded in success or failure, although he acts, he is not bound."
(Bhagavad Gita, 4;22)

4.

ॐ

kAyavAnmanah kAryamuttamam /
pUjanaMjapaScintanaM kramAt //

In the matter of worship, *japa* and meditation, which are performed by body, speech, and mind respectively ... each is better than the one before.

Notes

In this verse, three kinds of action are mentioned.

Worship is performed by the body so long as one considers oneself to be a separate entity. This attitude of 'otherness' has come about as a result of the limiting adjunct of self-consciousness and the ensuing fictional understanding of the mind/body complex. Worship of God is an appeal for return to unity and as such has great validity. However, **without due care**, it can atrophy into mere desire for boons, whether that be wealth, possessions, fame, enlightenment, etc. This type of worship is founded in ignorance. *PUja* degraded to this level of desire is wild fantasy. If the posture of the body, the dress of the body, the paraphernalia of worship, the fruit of worship, have become all important, while the object of worship has become of secondary consideration, then worship has become a farce. On the other hand, worship with the sole purpose of pleasing the object of worship (*ishta devatA*), without any desire for reward, becomes *upAsanA* (pure worship). This worship inevitably leads to *nididhyAsana*, uninterrupted contemplation, where 'otherness' is totally absent.

Better than physical worship is *japa. Japa* stills the mind by focussing on a single thought. When *japa* becomes mental and steady, *dhyAna* ensues. With the necessary development of dispassion for the visible universe, even one repetition has the power to transform.

"How can one reach liberation as a consequence of merely pronouncing the word *'Brahman'*, without having eliminated the visible universe, without having known the truth about one's own nature?" (Vivekacudamani, 63)

Better than *japa* is meditation. Meditation occupies the mind, channels the mind, and strengthens the mind in readiness for Self-enquiry. If it remains limited to the view of self and other, or subject and object, it remains useless, merely occupying the mind while still relying on the continued existence of the mind. By nature, this type of meditation is divisive, relying on set times and places for performance. However, concentrated continual meditation on the source of 'I' (*dhyAna*) is the meditation which opens the way to thought-free consciousness. This can, and should, be carried on throughout the day in all situations.

5.

ॐ

jagatISadhIyuktasevanam /
ashTamUrtibhrddevapUjanaM //

**Serving the world with intent on the Lord, is the worship
of the divine bearing the eight forms (earth, water, fire,
air, space, sun, moon, *jIva*).**

Notes

"Serving the world with intent on the Lord." Here worship as *upAsanA*, as opposed to a mere outward show of worship, is described. This is worship par excellence, free from conceptual diversification, free from desire for reward.

The Lord is everything and everything is the Lord. Whereas people 'normally' view 'things' as external, and other than themselves, realise instead that this is imagination, illusion, mindstuff. This world ... here and now ... is that one reality, the Self. There is nothing other than this. You should see this now, in all circumstances. This worship is eternal worship. This is seeing Actuality. *Brahman* worships *Brahman* by means of *Brahman*. When, just once, things are seen as they are ... no longer will the false be taken for reality. Sri Ramana teaches us to see the Self in everything, and everything in the Self.

It is not the case that you must give up your forms of worship but rather that you open to the truth as presented by great sages such as Sri Ramana. To falsely give up your *sAdhana* in the guise of a *jnani* is, in any case, useless. As long as the attitude of 'doer' remains, as long as you believe 'things' are real, so long is prayer and worship necessary. If you take on the attitude of the *jnani* without the Heart of a *jnani* your words and actions will be an anathema. Broaden your worship, keep your mind in worshipful attitude at all times. If the mind drifts pull it gently back. All things are in the Self, reliant on the Self. There is nothing without the Self. Being is, itSelf, worship. Sri Ramana says, "Keeping God in your mind as everything around you becomes *dhyAna*."

"To Love all is the true *bhakti* of God,
and to serve all is the real worship of God."
(Swami Ramdas)

6.

ॐ

uttamastavAduccamandatah /
cittajaMjapadhyAnamuttamam //

Meditation on *japa* born of mind is better than the best hymns of praise whether chanted loudly or softly.

Notes

Here real *japa* is described.

Parrot-like repetition, of a few sacred words, is not very effective without due meditation (although it has limited validity). The endless repetition of the Vedic hymns (or other scriptures) without care and due meditation, irrespective of the skill in utterance, may achieve personal acclaim and boost the ego of the narrator, but can never achieve liberation. Gross speech, whether mental or vocal, is totally reliant on thought. Without attention focussed on the source of thought (*paSyantI*), of the one who thinks, where is the point? On the other hand, how could a single utterance, made with complete understanding of its unique source, even although uttered wrongly (*apabrahmSa*), not have the power to reveal the ever-present *Sabdabrahman*?

How can it be possible to attain liberation simply by pronouncing the word 'God', without also seeking to know the essence of one's Self and thereby eliminating the visualised universe? Those who believe it possible have set off on the never ending search for the horn of the hare. You cannot become King simply by declaring "I am King!" You have to go out and defeat your enemies before taking hold of the country. Your enemies are thought-demons which dissipate your strength of mind. Eliminate them and then, indeed, just one word can pull you to the Heart-centre.

By all means (and at all times) ... pronounce the name of God ... but with care, with full attention, with reflection, and with due meditation. Rather than absent-minded repetition develop a present-minded disposition. The very name of God should become your Being. Speech comes from the Self. Speech is the Self. Speech returns to the Self. Watch it arise. Watch it subside. There is the source. Abide there. This is the elusive practice of *SabdapUrvayoga*.

When this becomes a continuous practice then *upAsana*, or *dhyAna*, becomes fixed.

7.

ॐ

AjyadhArayAsrotasAsamam /
saralacintanaM viralatah param //

As in the flow of ghee, as in the flow of a stream, an unbroken, true meditation is superior to one with intervals.

Notes

Here true meditation is described.

As ghee runs in a steady, deliberate, continuous stream when poured, so meditation should be steady, deliberate and continuous. As pure water always finds its way back to its source, irrespective of terrain, so the act of meditation should continue in an unbroken stream, with the sole aim of returning to the Source, overcoming all obstacles in its way.

Sri Ramana has stated that ... "Meditation is, truly speaking, *Atmanishtha* (to be fixed as the Self). But when thoughts cross the mind and an effort is made to eliminate them the effort is usually termed meditation. *Atmanishtha* is your true nature. Remain as you are. That is the true aim." (Talk 294)

When one becomes established in such deliberate meditation (*dhyAna*), it becomes the mind's natural predilection. Then like water the mind always eagerly flows to its source. The mind is then likened to a pure mountain spring ever rushing towards its source (goal).

Note: See also Sri Bhagavan's explanation under verse 13 below.

8.

ॐ

bhedabhAvanAt so'hamityasau /
bhAvanA'bhidA pAvanImatA //

Rather than promoting difference, the meditation, 'so-ham' ('I am He'), effects non-difference. This is considered purifying.

Notes

The mind becomes bound to the visualised universe and perpetuates its independent existence, in effect, by thinking 'I am not *Brahman*': The outward going mind, even in meditation, worships God as different from itself and continues to cling to its separate identity, content to give way during meditation only because it retains the sure knowledge that it will resume its independence on completion of meditation as a task (part of ego's 'doing' arsenal). Therefore one must eliminate this shortcoming and arrive at that understanding, which is neither theory, nor speculation, without resorting to conceptual thinking. In this way there comes about the realisation that we are the world and the world is us. In a previous verse Sri Ramana has stated that "serving the world with intent on the Lord is worship of the Divine", here another clue is given as to how this is effected. Meditation on 'soham' ('I am He') effects the realisation that the Self is each one of us and each one of us is the Self.

Note: The revealed *Mahavakyas* '*prajnanam Brahma*' ('Consciousness is *Brahman*'), from Aitareya Upanishad, reveals the nature of the Self; '*aham brahmasmi*' ('I am *Brahman*'), which is found in the Brihadaranyaka Upanishad reveals the source of the enquiry; 'tat tvam asi' ('That Thou Art') is found in the Chandogya Upanishad; this is the statement Guru Ramana reiterates again and again. '*Ayam Atma brahma*' ('This *Atman* is *Brahman*'), this is found in the Mandukya Upanishad; this identifies our very Being with *Brahman*.

9.

ॐ

bhAvaSUnyasad bhAvasusthitih /
bhavanAbalAd bhaktiruttamA //

A supreme devotion arises because of strength of meditation, an excellent state of Being which is devoid of appearances.

Notes:

That single reality (the Self) is devoid of all appearances and without differences; Existence ... without beginning or end; everywhere, endless, infinite; underlying all forms, all changes, all forces, all matter, all spirit. This is the state of Being.

Supreme *bhakti* is invigorated by the strength of meditation which is facilitated when the meditator and the object of meditation are not differentiated (as in the meditation so'ham). This *bhakti* is not different from *Atma vicAra* (Self-enquiry). Undoubtedly '...the Self of the Advaitins is the God of the *bhaktas*.' (Ramana Maharshi)

In *NAradabhaktisUtrANi*, *NArada* concurs when he proclaims, "now that (Supreme Devotion) comes about when one rejects the visible universe (the separation which validates seeing 'things' as objects of the ego) and completely renounces objective attachment." (*sUtra* 35) This *bhakti* is synonymous with Self-Realisation; it is devotion without desire; it is its own fruit, i.e. path and goal are one and the same.

10.

ॐ

hrtsthalemanah svasthatAkriyA /
bhaktiyogabodhAScaniScitam //

The act (*kriyA*) of abiding in one's natural state, the mind set in the Heart, is without doubt, Devotion, Yoga and Knowledge.

Notes:

Here, *kriyA* (action) refers to the one truly continuous, uncaused, meritorious 'act' (*kriyAyoga*). This is eternal Being, the Self. Where the mind finds this place (*dhyAna*), i.e. its place of birth, there is the culmination of *karma*, *bhakti*, *yoga*, and *jnana*. For the purified mind, this takes the form of constant remembrance, also called *nididhyAsana*. This is realisation of one's natural state. Referring to this verse Sri Bhagavan proclaims, **"That is the whole truth in a nut-shell."** (Talk 222)

In practice this may take the form of, daily attention to the silent murmur of the Self, pulling the mind back through Self-enquiry (the vibration ... 'I', 'I', 'I' ..., at times even becoming physically manifest on the right side of the chest), the abolition of *viyoga* through work/actions attended to selflessly, without desire for the fruits, or, the setting up of and perpetual remembrance of Sri Bhagavan in the temple of the Heart. The devotee, by Sri Bhagavan's Grace, often finds all of these in his/her life.

"*Swa swarupanusandhanam bhaktirityabhidhee-yate* (Reflection on one's own Self is called *bhakti*). *Bhakti* and Self-Enquiry are one and the same. The Self of the Advaitins is the God of the *bhaktas*." (Talk 274)

D.: What is *Jana Marga*?

M.: Concentration of the mind is in a way common to both Knowledge and *Yoga*. *Yoga* aims at union of the individual with the universal, the Reality. This Reality cannot be new. It must exist even now, and it does exist. Therefore the Path of Knowledge tries to find out how *viyoga* (separation) came about. The separation is from the Reality only. (Talk 17)

11.

ॐ

vAyurodhanAllIyatemanah /
jAlapakshivadrodhasAdhanam //

Through checking the breath, the mind cowers, like a bird caught in a net. This is a means of control.

Notes

Controlling the mind automatically controls the breath. However, for one who is unable to control the mind directly, Sri Ramana recommends breath control. Checking the breath causes the mind to falter.

Breath control is normally spoken of as having three stages: *rechaka* – exhalation; *pUraka* – inhalation; *kumbhaka* – retention.

In Talk 448, Sri Bhagavan has given the following instruction in *Jnana prAnAyama* (This is different from Hatha Yoga descriptions):

"Naham – I am not this – corresponds to *rechaka*
Koham – Who am I? (search for the I) – corresponds to *pUraka*
Soham – He am I (The Self alone) – corresponds to *kumbhaka*.
So these are the funktions of *prAnAyama*.
Again the three formulae are:
Na – *Aham* (Not – I).

Ka – *Aham* (Who – I).

Sa – *Aham* (He – I).

Delete the prefixes and hold on to the common factor in all of them. That is *Aham* – 'I', that is the gist of the whole matter."

This is a form of *Atma vicAra*.

PrAnAyama is also discussed in Yoga texts such as Siva Samhita, Gheranda Samhita, Hatha Yoga Pradipika and Yoga Sutras, among others. For those pursuing the path laid down by Sri Ramana, breath control is said to be of two kinds, *kevala kumbhaka* (absolute retention) and *prAnAyama* (regulation). The source of the breath is the same as the source of the mind therefore, when the breath subsides, so does the mind and, vice versa, when the mind subsides, so does the breath. *Kevala kumbhaka* overcomes all tendencies (*vAsanas*), mind becomes purified, and the flow of breath (life force: *prAna*) is established, spontaneously, in the *brahma nAdi*, which is, in essence, the Self. This is achieved by the method described previously by Sri Ramana and by His Grace.

PrAnAyama is an auxiliary practice which, like *japa*, meditation, etc., can prepare one for the direct path of Self-enquiry. If an aspirant cannot immediately take to Self-enquiry, then the mind should be directed to watch the flow of breath. This will bring about *kumbhaka* and control of mind.

For those who are unable to bring about *kumbhaka* by simply observing the outgoing and incoming breaths, Sri Ramana mentions *prAnAyama*, as propounded by the Hatha Yogis. The following ratio has been suggested: *rechaka*; *pUraka*; *kumbhaka* – 1; 1; 4 (cf. Ramana Gita, Chapter 6). Then, gradually, on purification of the channels (*nadis*), *Suddha kumbhaka* ensues (complete control of breath) and with such control one becomes established in the Source of thought.

However, the easiest and safest method is to simply persevere with the observance of the breath. This is very effective and can be done without the need of any supervision.

Note: It must be remembered that control of breath is a temporary/preparatory measure only. *Atma vicAra* is the final solution for eradication of the human condition. For those who cannot take to this Supreme Path straight away, control of breath brings one 'closer'.

12.

ॐ

cittavAyavaScitkriyAyutAh /
SAkhayordvayI SaktimUlakA //

Minds and breaths along with (their respective) thoughts and actions are two branching paths which spring from one inherent (potential) power.

Notes

Any number of branching paths, when traced back, always lead to a single source. That single innate source is the Self of all. All the senses lead back to that one source. Thoughts start from and end in that one source. Words arise from and return to that one source. The inherent power is that one source. The goal is ever the same, irrespective of the supposed starting point. The starting point is in reality also the goal.

Although *Sakti's* movement appears to bring words and worlds into being, the reality is that there is never any movement.

Whether thoughts float aimlessly or aimfully, that one source remains unaffected. Whether good actions or bad actions are performed, that one source remains unaffected. The potential can only be perceived, retrospectively, by the one who creates division. It is this dualistic vision which stimulates movement in the ground of Being. By understanding the source of thoughts and actions, one becomes firmly established in their source (*AtmanishTha*).

13.

ॐ

layavinASane ubhayarodhane /
layagatampunarbhavatinomrtam //

**Abeyance and destruction are the two types of control.
That which is in abeyance comes back again, not that
which is destroyed.**

Notes

Here, the term *'laya'* indicates that kind of mental inactivity that might be attained through hypnotism, faint or trance. It should also be noted that **'mature'** *vicAra* can, and will, cut to the source even in faint. This is the experience of some. However, as long as it cherishes its perceived (objective) independence, the mind retains that independence, even if the mental inactivity was to last for one hundred years. 'Happiness', thus achieved, lasts only so long as the inactivity lasts, then the old *vAsanas* (habits of the mind), which were merely dormant, return as before. Although this may be helpful, this is not the final solution.

The attempt to merely hold back these habitual, outgoing tendencies can never give anything other than temporary relief, followed by a resurgence of thought. Consider the inactivity experienced every day in deep sleep or even that experienced under anaesthetic. Instead, destruction (*vinASana*) is advocated. Only a **conscious quest** for the I-thought, the first (and last) of all thoughts, will resolve the human condition and result in *sahaja samAdhi*. *VicAra* must become the default state of mind throughout daily activity.

By *'vinASana'* (destruction or disappearance), permanent removal of the *vAsanas* is meant. This is achieved by rooting out the 'I'-thought once and for all. This is the real solution for the human condition.

27

"There are two kinds of *vasanas*: (1) *bandha hetuh*, causing bondage for the ignorant, and (2) *bhoga hetuh*, giving enjoyment for the wise. The latter do not obstruct realisation. (Talk 317)

Sri Bhagavan explained:

"Meditation should remain unbroken as a current. If unbroken it is called *samadhi* or *Kundalini sakti*.

The mind may be latent and merge in the Self; it must necessarily rise up again; after it rises up one finds oneself only as ever before. For in this state the mental predispositions are present there in latent form to remanifest under favourable conditions.

Again the mind activities can be totally destroyed. This differs from the former mind, for here the attachment is lost, never to reappear. Even though the man sees the world after he has been in the *samadhi* state, the world will be taken only as its worth, that is to say it is the phenomenon of the One Reality. The True Being can be realised only in *samadhi*; what was then is also now. Otherwise it cannot be Reality or Ever-present Being. What was in *samadhi* is here and now too. Hold it and it is your natural condition of Being. *Samadhi* practice must lead to it. Otherwise how can *nirvikalpa samadhi* be of any use in which a man remains as a log of wood? He must necessarily rise up from it sometime or other and face the world. But in *sahaja samadhi* he remains unaffected by the world." (Talk 465)

14.

ॐ

*prANabandhanAllInamAnasam /
ekacintanAnnASametyadah //*

Through control of breath, mind cowers. Through contemplation of one thought, it (mind) is destroyed.

Notes

"*Prana* and mind arise from the same source." (Talk 328)

As discussed at verse 11 above, control of breath automatically causes the mind to fall into inactivity. To destroy (or purify/purge) the mind, one-pointed contemplation, with the focus towards the root of the mind, is all that is required. This is *Atma jnana* (Knowledge of the Self).

"Bhagavan: *Eka chintana* involves continuous thought. If no other thought is to come, the one thought has to be continuous. What is meant by the verse is as follows. The previous verses have said that for controlling the mind breath-control or *pranayama* may be helpful. This verse says that the mind so brought under control or to the state of *laya* should not be allowed to be in mere *laya* or a state like sleep, but that it should be directed towards *eka chintana* or one thought, whether that one thought is of the Self, the *Ishta Devata* or a *mantram*. What the one thought may be, will depend on each man's *pakva* or fitness. The verse leaves it as one thought." (Day by Day with Bhagavan; 21-1-46)

15.

ॐ

nashTamAnasotkrshTayoginah /
krtyamastikim svasthitimyatah //

For the Great Yogi whose mind is destroyed, who abides in His own Self, is there anything to be done?

29

Notes

You have to brush all mental concepts aside to find out. The problem is identification with the wrong 'I' – the 'I'-thought – the source of the mind – the source of mentalese (the incessant chattering of the mind – 'mindstuff'). This 'I' rises and sets each day, even re-creates itself to suit the occasion. The Great Yogi on the other hand has no need to ask "Is there anything to be done?" He just gets on with it. With mind purged (purified), he is ready for anything. Here is a mind which begins, when necessary, fresh at all times, which is ever Self-sufficient (*purNa*) within itself. Here is a mind which is truly open. Free-flowing. Thriving in Self-dependence. Without achievement. Without thought of attainment. Without desire to do. Without projection. Without illusions of *dvaita* or *advaita* or any concoction in between. Here, then, is the mind without the binding thought of enlightenment. Here is your mind, purged, purified, Self-sufficient, spontaneous. This ... is available in your practice ... right now; at this very moment. Reflecting change, remaining unchanged. Being as it is.

mana eva manushyANAm kAraNam bandhamokshayoh /
bandhAya vishayAsaktam muktam nirvishayam smrtam //2//

"It is the mind, alone, that is the cause of people's bondage and liberation. One whose mind is devoted to the world (of objects) is bound. One whose mind is not devoted to the world (of objects) is liberated. So it is declared (by the wise)!"
(Amrtabindupanishad)

16.

ॐ

drSyavAritamcittamAtmanah /
cittvadarSanam tattva darSanam //

The mind, withheld from seeing the multiple universe, becomes the consciousness of the Self ... that is the vision of true wisdom.

Notes

True wisdom is not dependent on that which is seen, nor on that which is heard, nor on that which is tasted, nor on that which is touched. The consciousness of the Self is not dependent on any sense, yet all of the senses are dependent on the consciousness of the Self. This, withholding from seeing the multiple universe, is called *brahmacharya*. *Brahmacharya* is living with one's being entirely surrendered to *Brahman* or Self (Brahma – truth, *Brahman* – the absolute; *Carya* – conduct, practice of, occupation with). Earlier we spoke of "entirely giving up the notion of false 'I'." This is *brahmacharya*. By giving up *ahamkara*, the Truth is revealed. When you pander to the sense of sight ... you deny the Self. When you pander to the sense of hearing ...you deny the Self. When you pander to the sense of taste ... you deny the Self. When you pander to the sense of touch ...you deny the Self. As soon as you make an object of 'things' ... you deny the Self. This is the problem of the human condition. *Brahmacharya* is the effective antidote. If *brahmacharya* is adopted, the senses become conduits of the Self rather than slaves of the objective environment. The attitude, 'I am doing this', vanishes. This negation of the Self is counteracted by the truism of *brahmacharya*. The most effective means of achieving *brahmacharya* is by adopting the path of *Atma vicAra* (Self-enquiry). Then you can conduct yourself in a manner which is conducive to a life filled with True Wisdom. This is your innate being (*svabhAva*). This is true independence. Uniqueness. Now your life becomes spontaneous. The universe is seen for what it is.

yato nirvishayasyAsya manaso muktirishyate /
ato nirvishayam nityam manah kAryam mumukshuNa //3//

"Because liberation is assured for a mind which is not devoted to objects ... for that very reason, the mind should constantly be made free of attachment to objects, by one who aspires for liberation."
(Amrtabindupanishad)

17.

ॐ

mAnasamtukim mArgaNekrte /
naivamAnasam mArga ArjAvAt //

**However when the investigation is made into the mind,
there is no such mind. This is the expedient path, because
it is straight.**

Notes

How is this achieved?

"When an enquiry is made to find out what is the mind, that is, of what form it is, nothing like mind remains at the end. The enquirer himself is the true form of the mind. It is only his special ray, emanation. At the time of enquiry, the emanating ray converges in the Self. Then there is no mind at all. Thus teaches Bhagavan. This is the path as it is straight." (from the Muni's Bhashya. In: Bhagavan and Nayana, p. 51)

We are not advised to analyse the nature of the mind but rather look directly. ... In seeing directly all is answered.

Mind is to the snake what the Self is to the rope. The mind (as object) arises because there is identification of the Self with the body. There is mediation, where no mediation is required. We are not encouraged to analyse the mind but go straight to the root instead. Mind is simply the restlessness of the human condition. When it wanders, the world is created. In reality the mind is not an independent entity. Yet independence is assumed of it. "The mind is the outcome of the ego and the ego is from the Self." (Ramana Maharshi) No boundary separates the subjective from the objective yet it appears that mind attempts to fulfil such a role. In reality though, 'mind' (*manas*) simply provides fodder for philosophers' who dream of mind.

The expedient path is, by nature (*svabhAva*), devoid of diversification. A bird flies like a bird. A fish swims like a fish. Neither one tries to be the other nor for that matter does it even try to be itself. There is nothing more natural than abidance in the Self. Bhagavan delights in giving us the shortest route.

> "The mind is only a bundle of thoughts. The thoughts have their roots in the 'I'-thought. He quoted: 'Whoever investigates the origin of the 'I'-thought for him the ego perishes. This is true investigation.' The true 'I' is then found shining by itself." (Talk 222)

18.

ॐ

vrttayastvaham vrttimASritAh /
vrttayo mano viddhyahammanah //

All states of mind are dependent on the activity of the 'I'. The activities are the mind. Know that the 'I' is the mind.

Notes

Activities of mind are dependent on the pseudo-independent action and reaction of the ego applied to, produced by, and constantly creating situations. This inevitably leads to extreme viewpoints (opposites). On the one hand, the Self, eternally flowing from the Heart through everything, form and event, spontaneously expressing itself through itself; on the other hand the ego-self, blind with the illusion of separate existence and deaf to the voice from within, ever-striving for self, to the detriment of other, with 'freewill' battling against the universe, in a vain attempt to fulfil its purely personal desires. The 'I' models a narrow universe which suits its whims and desires. The subject 'I' predicates its 'happiness', 'sadness', 'cleverness', 'stupidity', 'love for this', 'hate for that'. This bundle of thoughts, for that is all mind is, this mindstuff, superimposes itself on *arUpa* (the formless). Then boxed within this self-created linear model based on 'relative knowledge' it lives happily, sadly, etc., etc., modifying constantly its 'known' universe. *NAma* (the naming game) is its occupation.

19.

ॐ

ahamayamkuto bhavaticinvatah /
ayipatatyaham nijavicAraNam //

"Where does this 'I' come from?" For one who enquires ...Aha! ... the 'I' falls away. This is Self-enquiry.

Notes

When, at last, one pursues Self-enquiry with single-minded devotion, the inevitable result is for the ego-'I' simply to fall away, defeated, destroyed, leaving a spontaneous iteration of one's true identity. All the 'stuff' that this 'I' had given substance to, vanishes in an instant. The subject/object relationship has shifted.

Atma vidya, the supreme science of self- knowledge, is the key. Simply by focussing intently on the root of this 'I', which inevitably appears in every situation, such as 'I think', 'I like', 'I hate', 'I am tall', 'I am small', 'I am important', 'I have a family', etc., the 'I' sense (ego) falls away and **I** ... remains. **I** remain complete, as always. The mind requires **I** ..., but **I** ... do not require the mind. **I** ... is the permanent substrate upon which all the states appear. Waking, dream, and deep sleep all share this common ground, this ground of Being.

In Self-enquiry all is resolved in one singe question, "Who am I?"

"D.: What is the practice?

M.: Constant search for 'I', the source of the ego. Find out 'Who am I?' The pure 'I' is the reality, the Absolute Existence-Conscousness-Bliss. When That is forgotten, all miseries crop up; when that is held fast, the miseries do not affect the person." (Talk 17)

Whenever one is distracted by thought ask "To whom does this thought appear?" The answer "To me" is then resolved with the question "Who am I?" This is not a question for the intellect. There is no answer. Any answer the intellect might give returns one to the question "To whom does this thought appear?" The questioner himself is the answer.

eka evAtmA mantavyo jAgratsvapnasushuptishu /
sthAnatrayavyatItasya punarjanma na vidyate //11//
"The *Atman* must be regarded as One and the same in waking, dream and dreamless sleep. For that One who has transcended the three states, rebirth does not exist."
(Amratindupanishad)

20.

ॐ

ahaminASabhAjyahamahamtayA /
sphuratihRtsvayam paramapUrNasat //

When the 'I' sense (ego) is destroyed, the Heart, as the supreme complete being (totality), spontaneously bursts forth (appears clearly), by itself as 'I'-'I'.

Notes

That supreme and complete Being is, because of its completeness (*purNa*), neither solely within nor solely without, but rather within and without (i.e. all there is), the true 'Centre without circumference'. The ego-'I' merely 'appears' as the limiting adjuncts. This 'I'

35

acts like a sheath which purports to contain that within which it, itself, is contained. Its source is, and has always been, That, which in one respect might be described as 'bursting forth' when it, the 'I' sense, perishes, or, in another respect, as 'throbbing' (beating), as Itself and by Itself, eternally, continuously, the Heart of all. This does not negate the empirical world but rather returns it to its rightful place as an uncaused appearance in *Brahman*.

That this, **'I'-'I'**, can be felt within the body, as the very vibration of being, should not be a surprise, nor should it appear incongruous, after all the body/mind's existence is entirely reliant on the Self. As an imaginary pot lying at the bottom of the ocean, must contain water and be immersed in water, so it is with the body. Should it therefore be impossible for the Self to express itself through this body? Now that would be incongruous. This idea, that the twin concepts 'spiritual' and 'material' are discrete units (i.e. that there are two 'I's, one spiritual and one material), is the sole illusion.

"The whole universe is in the body, the whole body is in the Heart; therefore the entire manifestation of the universe is contained in the Heart." (Ramana Gita)

21.

ॐ

idamahampadAbhikhyamanvaham /
ahamilInake 'pyalayasattayA //

This (i.e. the Heart) has the name 'I';
even if the 'I' (ego-sense) is completely absorbed, daily
(i.e. in deep sleep), still its real existence ('I'-'I') is never
destroyed.

Notes

"D.: *Aham* 'I' applies to the individual and also to *Brahman*. It is rather unfortunate.

M.: It is *upadhi bheda* (owing to different limiting adjuncts). The bodily limitations pertain to the *aham* ('I') of the *jiva*, whereas the universal limitations pertain to the *aham* ('I') of *Brahman*. Take off the *upadhi* (limiting adjunct); the 'I' (*aham*) is pure and single." (Talk 433, see also Talk 314)

The Heart is calling **'I'-'I'**. However, as long as the cloud-like mind asserts its identity as 'I', the Self, as **'I'-'I'**, although ever resounding, and most intimate, goes unnoticed, unfelt. The *upAdhis* are limiting factors which bring about the appearance of sequence and differentiation, starting with wrong association of 'I' with the inert mind/body complex. While the declaration 'I', by the ego, immediately brings 'my' and 'mine' in its wake, and then, in turn, 'you' and 'yours' etc. etc., this is solely because of the auspices of the primary, undifferentiated sole identity which throbs unceasingly, as the real **'I'-'I'**. As soon as the ego gives up its habit of Self-limitation, (through Self-enquiry), Heart to Heart speech, although deafeningly silent, is felt, vibrantly, as ever.

Sri Ramana's Teaching comes directly from the Heart ... and as such ... His words are an eternally vibrant and living compassion. If we open to Sri Ramana's words, Heart speaks to Heart, and the head (intellect) falls naturally in perpetual *namaskAr*.

om sri gurave namah

22.

ॐ

vigrahendriya prANadhItamah /
nAhamekasattajjaDamhyasat //

This sole existent 'I' is not the delusion of (separation into) body, senses, breath, and mind. That (delusion) is insentient, non-existent (untrue).

Notes

D.: Why does Upadesa Sara speak of the body, etc., as *jaDa* i.e. insentient?

M.: Inasmuch as you say that they are the body, etc., apart from the Self. But when the Self is found this body, etc., are also found to be in it. Afterwards no one will ask the question and no one will say that they are insentient. (Talk 310)

Self-limitation is epitomised in the delusion which creates the division of ego-self and 'all' others and continues with further divisions such as body, senses, breath and mind etc. The mind-made delusion is unreal, insentient, mindstuff. While both the Sage and the ignorant man might declare, 'I am the body', the ignorant man, in separation, limits his 'concrete idea' of self to the mind and body alone whereas the Sage understands that 'all', including mind and body, is entirely dependent on the Self alone. For the Sage the world is real because he sees that it partakes of, and is reliant on, the Being-ness of the One existent Self alone, unconditioned, unborn and non-dual. In this way the Sage affirms, rather than denies, Reality. However the ignorant man sees the world as a separate reality, as something other than the Self (e.g. as if he swears that the silver in the mother of pearl has a real and separate, independent existence), and sets up divisions within himself and also within the world he 'observes'. His divisions are not limited by self and world but extend to the spiritual and material. This is *jaDa*, unintelligent. The falsehood of separation results in the human condition. Mind then moulds his creation. Separation is the attitude of ignorance. If you see yourself as separate from others and others as separate from you then you sustain the multiple fields of selfish action and the resultant 'fruits' which appear to arise. Whereas if, like the Sage, one considers that the creation of the world never happened and affirms that, in absolute terms, it is an uncaused appearance, action reverts to spontaneous Self-expression.

D.: Should I not see the world at all?

M.: You are not instructed to shut your eyes from the world. You are only to 'see yourself first and then see the whole world as the Self'. If you consider yourself as the body the world appears to be external. If you are the Self the world appears as *Brahman*. (Talk 272)

23.

ॐ

sattvabhAsikAcit kvavetarA /
sattayAhicit cittayAhyaham //

How can one say that another consciousness is illuminating Existence, when consciousness is of the nature of Existence (Self), and the 'I' is of the nature of consciousness?

Notes

Undivided, full and complete (*purNa*), Self-luminous, this Consciousness is the substratum of existence. All else is totally dependent on It.

M.: The whole universe is full of life. You say the stone is unconscious. It is your self-consciousness which now speaks of unconsciousness. When a person wants to see if there is an article in a dark room he takes a lamp to look for it. The light is useful for detecting the presence and the absence of the thing. Consciousness is necessary for discovering if a thing is conscious or not. If a man remains in a dark room one need not take a lamp to find him. If called, he answers. He does not require a lamp to announce his presence. Consciousness is thus self-shining. (Talk 591)

The problem is the erroneous idea that the body is the 'I'. The real 'I' is always here. It neither comes nor goes. It is not reliant on the body. It pre-exists the body. It continues once the body has vanished. This is even evidenced in the daily pattern of the three states. The illusion, of multiple discrete consciousnesses, appears with the ghost of ego. This brings association with objects in its train. On the other hand, Consciousness is self-shining. It is pure Reality without need of associates. No other can recognise Consciousness save Consciousness itself. It is Oneness. Consciousness unconceived is the Absolute. Consciousness conceived is the Universe. Consciousness is one only, without a second.

Consciousness is expressed in the three states of waking, dream and deep, dreamless sleep. It is the *Atman*, Self, witness of all. Without Consciousness nothing can be conceived of.

Atma vicAra drives us home to the goal, where even witnessing is subsumed by the *Atman*, shining as It is, devoid of *upAdhis*. Self-enquiry reaveals the Truth.

D.: But is it not funny that the 'I' should be searching for the 'I'? Does not the enquiry, 'Who am I?' turn out in the end an empty formula? Or, am I put the question to myself endlessly, repeating it like some *mantra*?

M.: Self-enquiry is certainly not an empty formula; it is more than repetition of any *mantra*. If the enquiry, 'Who am I?' were a mere mental questioning, it would not be of much value. The very purpose of Self-enquiry is to focus the entire mind at its Source. It is not, therefore, a case of one 'I' searching for another 'I'.

Much less is Self-enquiry an empty formula, for it involves an intense activity of the entire mind to keep it steadily poised in pure Self-awareness. Self-enquiry is the one, infallible means, the only direct one, to realize the unconditioned, absolute Being that you really are. (Maharshi's Gospel, p. 37f)

24.

ॐ

ISajIvayorveshadhIbhidA /
satsvabhAvato vastukevalam //

Between God and *jIva* the difference is simply the thought of an assumed appearance. The real essence is one only, the state of Self-existence.

Notes

The basis of the many polemical arguments revolve around the perceived differences between God, *jIva* and the world. While these make for interesting academic debates and might spark off coffee shop philosophy they are of no use to the serious seeker. Lay all thought of difference aside (even that of *dvaita* and *advaita*). Find out about your own reality first.

The *jIva* is self-limited by his understanding of the universe. He plots this universe around his own self-centre which continually relates back to the known. Therefore his understanding must always be rooted in the past. He also posits a myriad 'other' self-centres which he clearly sees as 'not me'. As such, a universe of judgements and comparisons is created and sustained. Reality is seldom seen, except through a mist of assumptions and when at times it shines through as non-separative consciousness the immediate response is to enjoy, analyse or re-create, in effect to claim the event as 'mine', and thus relegate that which is constant, reality, to the level of relative experience. Immediately memory steals the moment and plots it for use as a basis for future judgements and comparisons.

God on the other hand is the ultimate Centre without circumference (i.e. without limitation). Unique. All-encompassing. All the dependent self-centres assume their places as sets and subsets within the Universal. God remains, as ever, immutable. This Centre is the true Centre of all. It defies definition. All points converge, here, in this Centre. And this Centre sustains all points. This should be the object of your meditation/quest.

> "The centre of the ego and its core is called the Heart, the same as the Self." (Talk 398)

25.

ॐ

veshahAnatah svAtmadarSanam /
ISadarSanam svAtmarUpatah //

By the elimination of assumed appearances, there is the vision of one's Self. This is the vision of God, because He is the form of one's own Self.

Notes

As we have seen the assumption of a false sense of selfhood and the setting up of oneself as the centre of the universe results in the human condition. The snake is seen as such only until true vision is brought to bear on the situation ... then the rope is revealed as the rope it always was. The appearances and their multitudinous explanations are mere polemics. Concentrate on the task at hand. True knowledge consists in distinguishing the Self, which is real, from the not Self, which is unreal.

"On enquiry into its seemingly reality the false world is seen to be as unreal as a snake in a mural painting. Even so, to practice penance or perform rituals (in order to force the world out of view), is like beating a drum to scare away the post mistaken for the thief. If the teaching 'All this is false' appears faultless to you and you know it to be true, why go in search of further knowledge? The dense darkness of ignorance having fled before the sun of knowledge, why do you still doubt if this is the true light?" (Ozhivil Odukkam)

"It is the Self which speaks of the non-self because it has forgotten itself. Having lost hold of itself, it conceives something as non-self, which is after all nothing but itself." (Talk 310)

26.

ॐ

Atmasamsthitih svAtmadarSanam /
AtmanirdvayAdAtmanishThatA //

Remaining as the Self is the vision of one's true nature.
Since there are not two selves, there is only Self-abidance.

Notes

To abide as the Self is all that is required.

"All this is *Brahman*." When the appearances, which constitute the human condition and its associates, dissolve, that which remains am 'I'. When these appearances drop away, the ever-existent Self remains, as always, as 'I'. This is the simple Truth. There is nothing new to be attained, there is no far off day or place when this will be achieved. There is no achievement as such but rather a dropping of the desire to achieve.

"The 'I' which rises will also subside. That is the individual 'I' or the 'I'-concept. That which does not rise will not subside. It *is* and will be forever. That is the universal 'I', the perfect 'I', or realisation of the Self." (Talk 311)

"You are always that. No matter how far and for how long you travel you can never ever travel any further from, or any nearer to, that. This is the simple truth. "It requires no effort, no aid. One has to leave off the wrong identity and be in his eternal, natural, inherent state." (Talk 101)

All suffering is reliant on the ignorance of the one fundamental fact that **"there are not two selves, there is only Self-abidance."** Misunderstanding this, all is misunderstood. Then self and other emanate relentlessly from our own consciousness.

27.

ॐ

jnAnavarjitAjnAnahInacit /
jnAnamastikim jnAtumantaram //

True knowledge is that understanding which is without (objective) knowledge or non-knowledge. What else is there to know?

Notes

The Self is sometimes said to be unknowable. By this is meant that objective knowledge is absent because other than the Self there is nothing else to be known. A pure mind has immediate access to this knowledge because it is devoid of thought. *Atma vicAra* keeps the mind free of thoughts.

"Sri Bhagavan said that it [the world] is unreal if viewed apart from the Self and real if viewed as the Self." (Talk 516)

44

'True knowledge' is the daily experience. When one interacts with the world the Self simply appears to take on myriad forms. Whether or not such forms are withdrawn the Self rests happily in itself. Nothing is gained, nothing is lost, whether the world is perceived, or not.

> "The *ajnani* takes the world to be real; whereas the *jnani* sees it only as the manifestation of the Self. It is immaterial if the Self manifests itself or ceases to do so." (Talk 65)

28.

ॐ

kim svarUpamityAtmadarSane /
avyayAbhavApUrNacitsukham //

If there is the vision of the Self, by enquiring "what is one's true form?", there is Self-fulfilled consciousness-bliss which is without beginning and end.

Notes

"Who am I? Whence am I?" This is the enquiry! It is an enquiry into the source of the 'I'-thought. There is no answer that ego can offer that would not result in a return to the self-same Quest. When the real answer arises spontaneously there is absolutely no doubt!

> "The thought 'I', 'mine' erroneously imposed on the body and senses, which are not the real self, must be removed by the wise, by abiding as the real Self." (Vivekacudamani)

The universe of experience, to which the individual awakens each day, is reliant on the mind/body complex and dies with the disappearance of the mind/body complex. It has its beginning in birth and its end in death. Once born we become the centre of a world of our own making. This daily coming and going disappears in deep sleep, yet we remain.

"We exist in *sushupti* without being associated with the body and mind. But in the other two states [waking and dream] we are associated with them. If one with the body, how can we exist without the body in *sushupti*? We can separate ourselves from that which is external to us and not from that which is one with us. Hence the ego is not one with the body. This must be realised in the waking state. *Avasthatraya* (the three states of waking, dream and deep sleep) should be studied for gaining this outlook." (Talk 286)

"I am the Self, O Gudakesa, abiding in the hearts of all beings, I am the beginning, the middle and also the end of all beings." (Bhagavad Gita, 10; 20)

Beings go through their cycles of existence, of birth and death, of beginnings and ends, with no more substance than the participants in a dream. The true form of the Self, meanwhile, remains, as ever, as Being-Consciousness-Bliss.

29.

ॐ

bandhamuktyatItamparamsukham /
vindatIhajIvastudaivikah //

**Now, in this world, the divine soul attains the Supreme
Bliss which transcends bondage and liberation.**

Notes

Following on from the last verse, Sri Bhagavan reveals the true purport, i.e. that realisation is not to be attained at some distant appointment designated by fate but rather that it is not only available now, here, in this world (*iha*), but is, indeed, already here. In fact, to imagine a future enlightenment is a fundamental problem.

"*Muki*, i.e., liberation, is not to be gained hereafter. It is there forever, here and now. ... Existence=happiness=Being. The word *mukti* (liberation) is so provoking. Why should one seek it? He believes that there is bondage and therefore seeks liberation. But the fact is that there is no bondage but only liberation. Why call it by a name and seek it? ... Only remove ignorance. That is all there is to be done." (Talk 359)

The twin concepts, bondage and liberation are themselves limiting factors firmly entrenched in the world of opposites. Throughout this Upanishad [of Upadesa Saram] we have been reminded again and again by Bhagavan, that all that we must do is "first know our Self and then all other matters will be plain to us." (Talk 548) If we can but remain as our Self all is revealed, then liberation and bondage have nothing to do with our Being. First we must pay attention to the simple fact that Supreme Bliss transcends all thought of bondage and liberation. We must realise the full implication of this statement *Atma vicAra* is the appropriate and expedient (*yoga*) tool.

30.

ॐ

ahamapetakamnijavibhAnakam /
mahadidam tapo ramaNavAgiyam //

The perception of one's own Self, free of 'I', is the great *tapas*. This is Sri Ramana's word.

Notes

As we have noted the Enquiry is an enquiry into the source of *ahamkAra*. The Self needs no enquiry. All that is required is an emptying of the cloud-like thought processes which begin with the 'I'-thought. The senses can only perceive by the light they receive from the Self which abides in the Heart. The great *tapas*, which might at one time be seen as a penance sustained by great effort, is in reality the effortless return to the eternal fire of the *Atman* in the Heart.

"One-pointedness is the *tapas* wanted."(Talk 401)

The *tapas* of the Sages of DArukAvana was designed to appropriate power, through ritual (*karma*). But this merely reinforces *ahamkAra* and panders to the chronic desires with result in the human condition. In **Upadesa Saram**, Sri Bhagavan reveals that true *tapas* is nothing other than the perception of one's own Self. *Tapas* is the eternal flame which burns in the heart-cave of all. If we can but quieten the ego and turn towards it in *namaskAra*, all *vAsanas* are burned, in an instant.

om namo bhagavate sri ramanaya

"D.: What is *namaskara* (prostration)?
M.: Prostration means 'subsidence of the ego'. What is 'subsidence'? To merge in the source of its origin. God cannot be deceived by outward genuflections, bowings and prostrations. He sees if the idividuality is there or not." (Talk 363)

Glossary

abhimAna: attachment; self-conceit; pride
advaita: non-duality; unique; a school of philosophy
aham: I
ahamkAra: the 'I'-maker; ego-self; self-consciousness; concept of individuality
ajnani: the ignorant, one who has not realized the Self
amrta: blissful; immortal
Ananda: bliss; happiness; one of the three attributes of the Self (sat, cit ananda – Being, Consciousness and Bliss)
apabhramSa: fallen word; corrupt form
arUpa: formless
Atma(n): Self; *Brahman*; the Absolute
AtmanishTha: abidance in the Self
Atma vicAra: Self-enquiry
Atma vidya: knowledge of the Self
bandha hetuh: cause of bondage
bhakta: devotee
bhakti: devotion
bhoga hetuh: cause of pleasure
brahmacharya: [traditionally] celibacy; here it is used in the sense of 'complete occupation with *Brahman*'
brahma naAdi: nAdis are suble nerves (channels) described in Yoga texts; brahma nAdi, also referred as amrta nAdi, is the inner-most channel which is blissful and is, indeed, the Self
Brahman: the Supreme Being; the Absolute
dhyAna: meditation
dRSyavilayam: dispassion for the visible universe; dissolution of the universe
dvaita: duality; duplicity; a school of philosophy
eka chintana: one thought
ishta devatA: the deity chosen for worship or contemplation
jaDa: inert
japa: repetition of a *mantra* or sacred words such as 'om namo bhagavate sri ramanaya' under one's breath
jIva: the embodied self
jnana: knowledge

jana mArga: the path of knowledge

jnani: knower of the Self; Sage

karma: action; work; fruit of work

"Give up the sense of doership. *Karma* will go on automatically. Or *karma* will drop away from you. If *karma* be your lot according to *prarabhda,* it will surely be done whether you will it or not; if *karma* be not your lot, it will not be done even if you intently engage in it." (Talk 41)

Kartr: one who acts

kevala kumbhakta: absolute retention of breath

kriyA: practice

kriyAyoga: spontaneous action; abidance in the Self during everyday life

kumbhaka: retention of breath

Kundalini: The yogic power, as serpent, which traverses the yogic centres of the body; the Self

Laya: dissolution

Mahavakyas: "The Great Sayings" of the Upanishads

Manas: mind

mantra(m): sacred word; sacred text; incantation

mArga: path

mukti: liberation; spiritual freedom

nAma: name; name of God; the separation/creation of the world by the individual (the naming game)

namaskAr(a): prostration before God or Guru; surrender of the ego

NArada: the Sage who composed Narada Bhakti Sutras

NAradabhaktisUtrANi: Narada Bhakti Sutras, a devotional text composed by NArada

nididhyAsana: profound, unbroken meditation

nirvikalpa: free from distinctions

niyama: natural laws

pakva: fitness; maturity

paSyantI: the shining one; the first stage of speech

prAna: life force; breath; energy

pranayama: regulation of breathing

prarabhda: the part of one's *karma* which is to be worked out in this life

prayatna: effort

pUja: ceremonial worship with various paraphernalia

pUraka: inhalation

purNa: complete; full

purusha: man; God

Purva Karma: the doctrine of the Purva Mimamsas. They follow the Karma Kanda of the Veda. They are solely concerned with correct action in accordance with dharma (the order of the universe).

Rechaka: exhalation

Rishi: a seer; a sage

Sabdabrahman: unmanifest word *Brahman*; Om; the Self externalised in the Veda; *paSyantI*

SabdapUrvayoga: a method of tracing the mind back to its source; union with that which is before words, *Atma vicAra*

sAdhana: spiritual practice

sahaja: natural; the natural state

Sakti: power; potential

samAdhi: state of awareness; bringing into harmony; trance

sAram: nectar; essence

so'ham: sah aham, I am He

sphurana: the indefinable but palpable manifestation of the Self, which is felt at times all over but ultimately in the Heart centre

sUtra: string; aphorism

Suddha: Pure

Sushupti: dreamless sleep

svabhAva: one's own state of being; innateness; nature

svarUpa: own form; nature; essence

tapas: austerity

upadesa: spiritual instruction

Upadesa Saram: Nectar/Essence of Spiritual Instruction

upAdhi: limitation; limiting adjunct

upAsana: remaining close by; divine service; complete worship; worship of the Lord in His eightfold form

vAsana: habit; latent tendencies; mindstuff

vicAra: enquiry

vidya: knowledge

vinASana: destruction; disappearance

viyoga: separation

yoga: union (of *jIva* with *Brahman*); method; practice

Bibliography

Amrtabindu Upanishad, transl. from Sanskrit:
http://de.feedbooks.com/userbook/24278/amrtabindu-upanishad

The Collected Works of Ramana Maharshi. – 9th rev. ed. - Tiruvannamalai, 2004

Maharshi's Gospel: The Teachings of Sri Ramana Maharshi. - 14th
ed. – Tiruvannamalai, 2003

Mudaliar, A. Devaraja: Day by Day with Bhagavan. – 5th reprint. –
Tiruvannamalai, 2002

Shankaranarayanan, S.: Bhagavan and Nayana. - Tiruvannamalai,
1997

Sri Ramana Gita : The Teachings of Bhagavan Sri Ramana Maharshi. – Tiruvannamalai, 2003

Talks with Sri Ramana Maharshi. – 9th ed. – Tiruvannamalai, 1994